AF444033
This Bucket list belong to:

My Bucket List Goal

Date _________________ Location _________________

Reason of doing this:

Actions we have to take:

My Experience:

My Bucket List Goal

Date ___________   Location ___________

Reason of doing this:

Actions we have to take:

My Experience:

My Bucket List Goal

Date _______________ Location _______________

Reason of doing this:

Actions we have to take:

My Experience:

My Bucket List Goal

Date ________________ Location ________________

Reason of doing this:

Actions we have to take:

My Experience:

My Bucket List Goal

Date _____________   Location _____________

Reason of doing this:

____

____

____

____

Actions we have to take:

____

____

____

____

My Experience:

____

____

____

My Bucket List Goal

Date   Location

Reason of doing this:

Actions we have to take:

My Experience:

My Bucket List Goal

Date ___________ Location ___________

Reason of doing this:

____
____
____
____

Actions we have to take:

____
____
____
____
____

My Experience:

____
____
____

My Bucket List Goal

Date .... Location ....

Reason of doing this:

Actions we have to take:

My Experience:

My Bucket List Goal

Date _____________   Location _____________

Reason of doing this:

Actions we have to take:

My Experience:

My Bucket List Goal

Date ________________ Location ________________

Reason of doing this:

Actions we have to take:

My Experience:

My Bucket List Goal

Date ____________ Location ____________

Reason of doing this:

Actions we have to take:

My Experience:

My Bucket List Goal

Date _______________ Location _______________

Reason of doing this:

Actions we have to take:

My Experience:

My Bucket List Goal

Date ___________   Location ___________

Reason of doing this:

Actions we have to take:

My Experience:

My Bucket List Goal

Date _______________ Location _______________

Reason of doing this:

Actions we have to take:

My Experience:

My Bucket List Goal

Date _______________ Location _______________

Reason of doing this:

Actions we have to take:

My Experience:

My Bucket List Goal

Date _______________ Location _______________

Reason of doing this:

Actions we have to take:

My Experience:

My Bucket List Goal

Date   Location

Reason of doing this:

Actions we have to take:

My Experience:

My Bucket List Goal

Date ________________ Location ________________

Reason of doing this:

Actions we have to take:

My Experience:

My Bucket List Goal

Date ____________   Location ____________

Reason of doing this:

Actions we have to take:

My Experience:

My Bucket List Goal

Date _______________ Location _______________

Reason of doing this:

Actions we have to take:

My Experience:

My Bucket List Goal

Date ____________   Location ____________

Reason of doing this:

Actions we have to take:

My Experience:

My Bucket List Goal

Date .... Location ....

Reason of doing this:

Actions we have to take:

My Experience:

My Bucket List Goal

Date _______________ Location _______________

Reason of doing this:

Actions we have to take:

My Experience:

My Bucket List Goal

Date .... Location ....

Reason of doing this:

Actions we have to take:

My Experience:

My Bucket List Goal

Date _______________ Location _______________

Reason of doing this:

Actions we have to take:

My Experience:

My Bucket List Goal

Date _______________ Location _______________

Reason of doing this:

Actions we have to take:

My Experience:

My Bucket List Goal

Date _______________ Location _______________

Reason of doing this:

Actions we have to take:

My Experience:

My Bucket List Goal

Date .... Location ....

Reason of doing this:

Actions we have to take:

My Experience:

My Bucket List Goal

Date _____________ Location _____________

Reason of doing this:

Actions we have to take:

My Experience:

My Bucket List Goal

Date _____________ Location _____________

Reason of doing this:

Actions we have to take:

My Experience:

My Bucket List Goal

Date ______________ Location ______________

Reason of doing this:

Actions we have to take:

My Experience:

My Bucket List Goal

Date   Location

Reason of doing this:

Actions we have to take:

My Experience:

My Bucket List Goal

Date ___________   Location ___________

Reason of doing this:

Actions we have to take:

My Experience:

My Bucket List Goal

Date ______________   Location ______________

Reason of doing this:

____
____
____
____

Actions we have to take:

____
____
____
____
____

My Experience:

____
____
____
____

My Bucket List Goal

Date ___________   Location ___________

Reason of doing this:

Actions we have to take:

My Experience:

My Bucket List Goal

Date _______________ Location _______________

Reason of doing this:

Actions we have to take:

My Experience:

My Bucket List Goal

Date _______________ Location _______________

Reason of doing this:

Actions we have to take:

My Experience:

My Bucket List Goal

Date _____________ Location _____________

Reason of doing this:

Actions we have to take:

My Experience:

My Bucket List Goal

Date ______________ Location ______________

Reason of doing this:

Actions we have to take:

My Experience:

My Bucket List Goal

Date ______________________ Location ______________________

Reason of doing this:

Actions we have to take:

My Experience:

My Bucket List Goal

Date _____________   Location _____________

Reason of doing this:

Actions we have to take:

My Experience:

My Bucket List Goal

Date ___________________ Location _______________

Reason of doing this:

____

____

____

____

Actions we have to take:

____

____

____

____

____

My Experience:

____

____

____

My Bucket List Goal

Date ______________ Location ______________

Reason of doing this:

Actions we have to take:

My Experience:

My Bucket List Goal

Date _______________ Location _______________

Reason of doing this:

Actions we have to take:

My Experience:

My Bucket List Goal

Date ____________ Location ____________

Reason of doing this:

Actions we have to take:

My Experience:

My Bucket List Goal

Date ________________ Location ________________

Reason of doing this:

Actions we have to take:

My Experience:

My Bucket List Goal

Date _______________ Location _______________

Reason of doing this:

Actions we have to take:

My Experience:

My Bucket List Goal

Date .... Location ....

Reason of doing this:

Actions we have to take:

My Experience:

My Bucket List Goal

Date _______________   Location _______________

Reason of doing this:

Actions we have to take:

My Experience:

My Bucket List Goal

Date ______________________   Location ______________________

Reason of doing this:

____

____

____

____

Actions we have to take:

____

____

____

____

____

My Experience:

____

____

____

____

My Bucket List Goal

Date ____________________ Location ____________________

Reason of doing this:

Actions we have to take:

My Experience:

My Bucket List Goal

Date ________________ Location ________________

Reason of doing this:

Actions we have to take:

My Experience:

My Bucket List Goal

Date _______________ Location _______________

Reason of doing this:

Actions we have to take:

My Experience:

My Bucket List Goal

Date _______________ Location _______________

Reason of doing this:

Actions we have to take:

My Experience:

My Bucket List Goal

Date ______________   Location ______________

Reason of doing this:

Actions we have to take:

My Experience:

My Bucket List Goal

Date .... Location ....

Reason of doing this:

Actions we have to take:

My Experience:

My Bucket List Goal

Date ____________________   Location ____________________

Reason of doing this:

Actions we have to take:

My Experience:

My Bucket List Goal

Date _______________ Location _______________

Reason of doing this:

Actions we have to take:

My Experience:

My Bucket List Goal

Date ____________________ Location ____________________

Reason of doing this:

Actions we have to take:

My Experience:

My Bucket List Goal

Date .... Location ....

Reason of doing this:

Actions we have to take:

My Experience:

My Bucket List Goal

Date ________________ Location ________________

Reason of doing this:

Actions we have to take:

My Experience:

My Bucket List Goal

Date ____________________ Location ____________________

Reason of doing this:

Actions we have to take:

My Experience:

My Bucket List Goal

Date ________________ Location ________________

Reason of doing this:

Actions we have to take:

My Experience:

My Bucket List Goal

Date ______________ Location ______________

Reason of doing this:

Actions we have to take:

My Experience:

My Bucket List Goal

Date _______________ Location _______________

Reason of doing this:

Actions we have to take:

My Experience:

My Bucket List Goal

Date _____________ Location _____________

Reason of doing this:

Actions we have to take:

My Experience:

My Bucket List Goal

Date ______________ Location ______________

Reason of doing this:

Actions we have to take:

My Experience:

My Bucket List Goal

Date   Location

Reason of doing this:

Actions we have to take:

My Experience:

My Bucket List Goal

Date ___________________ Location ___________________

Reason of doing this:

____

____

____

____

Actions we have to take:

____

____

____

____

____

My Experience:

____

____

____

____

My Bucket List Goal

Date ______________ Location ______________

Reason of doing this:

Actions we have to take:

My Experience:

My Bucket List Goal

Date ____________ Location ____________

Reason of doing this:

____

____

____

____

Actions we have to take:

____

____

____

____

____

My Experience:

____

____

____

____

My Bucket List Goal

Date ____________________ Location ____________________

Reason of doing this:

Actions we have to take:

My Experience:

My Bucket List Goal

Date _______________ Location _______________

Reason of doing this:

Actions we have to take:

My Experience:

My Bucket List Goal

Date .... Location ....

Reason of doing this:

Actions we have to take:

My Experience:

My Bucket List Goal

Date ____________   Location ____________

Reason of doing this:

Actions we have to take:

My Experience:

My Bucket List Goal

Date

Location

Reason of doing this:

Actions we have to take:

My Experience:

My Bucket List Goal

Date ___________________ Location ___________________

Reason of doing this:

Actions we have to take:

My Experience:

My Bucket List Goal

Date _____________ Location _____________

Reason of doing this:

Actions we have to take:

My Experience:

My Bucket List Goal

Date ________________ Location ________________

Reason of doing this:

Actions we have to take:

My Experience:

My Bucket List Goal

Date   Location

Reason of doing this:

Actions we have to take:

My Experience:

My Bucket List Goal

Date ________________ Location ________________

Reason of doing this:

Actions we have to take:

My Experience:

My Bucket List Goal

Date ____________ Location ____________

Reason of doing this:

____

____

____

____

Actions we have to take:

____

____

____

____

My Experience:

____

____

____

____

My Bucket List Goal

Date _______________ Location _______________

Reason of doing this:

Actions we have to take:

My Experience:

My Bucket List Goal ____________________

____

Date __________________ Location __________________

Reason of doing this:

____

____

____

____

Actions we have to take:

____

____

____

____

My Experience:

____

____

____

____

My Bucket List Goal

Date ___________   Location ___________

Reason of doing this:

Actions we have to take:

My Experience:

My Bucket List Goal

Date .... Location ....

Reason of doing this:

Actions we have to take:

My Experience:

My Bucket List Goal

Date _______________ Location _______________

Reason of doing this:

Actions we have to take:

My Experience:

My Bucket List Goal ________

Date ________ Location ________

Reason of doing this:

____

____

____

____

Actions we have to take:

____

____

____

____

My Experience:

____

____

____

____

My Bucket List Goal

Date   Location

Reason of doing this:

Actions we have to take:

My Experience:

My Bucket List Goal

Date ______________________   Location ______________________

Reason of doing this:

Actions we have to take:

My Experience:

My Bucket List Goal

Date _______________ Location _______________

Reason of doing this:

Actions we have to take:

My Experience:

My Bucket List Goal

Date ____________________   Location ____________________

Reason of doing this:

Actions we have to take:

My Experience:

My Bucket List Goal

Date _____________ Location _____________

Reason of doing this:

Actions we have to take:

My Experience:

My Bucket List Goal

Date _____________ Location _____________

Reason of doing this:

Actions we have to take:

My Experience:

My Bucket List Goal

Date _______________ Location _______________

Reason of doing this:

Actions we have to take:

My Experience:

My Bucket List Goal

Date   Location

Reason of doing this:

Actions we have to take:

My Experience:

My Bucket List Goal

Date ____________ Location ____________

Reason of doing this:

Actions we have to take:

My Experience:

My Bucket List Goal

Date _________________ Location _________________

Reason of doing this:

Actions we have to take:

My Experience:

My Bucket List Goal

Date _______________ Location _______________

Reason of doing this:

Actions we have to take:

My Experience:

My Bucket List Goal

Date _______________ Location _______________

Reason of doing this:

Actions we have to take:

My Experience:

My Bucket List Goal

Date _______________ Location _______________

Reason of doing this:

Actions we have to take:

My Experience:

My Bucket List Goal

Date _______________ Location _______________

Reason of doing this:

Actions we have to take:

My Experience:

My Bucket List Goal

Date ___________________ Location ___________________

Reason of doing this:

Actions we have to take:

My Experience:

My Bucket List Goal

Date .... Location ....

Reason of doing this:

Actions we have to take:

My Experience:

My Bucket List Goal

Date   Location

Reason of doing this:

Actions we have to take:

My Experience:

My Bucket List Goal ......

Date ...... Location ......

Reason of doing this:

Actions we have to take:

My Experience:

My Bucket List Goal

Date ____________ Location ____________

Reason of doing this:

Actions we have to take:

My Experience:

My Bucket List Goal

Date _____________ Location _____________

Reason of doing this:

Actions we have to take:

My Experience: